CUMBRIA LIBRARIES

D0358971

Comparing Past and Present

Playing with Friends

Rebecca Rissman

Raintree

Raintree is an imprint of Capstone Global Library Limited, a company incorporated in England and Wales having its registered office at 7 Pilgrim Street, London, EC4V 6LB – Registered company number: 6695582

www.raintreepublishers.co.uk
myorders@raintreepublishers.co.uk

Text © Capstone Global Library Limited 2014
First published in hardback in 2014
The moral rights of the proprietor have been asserted.

All rights reserved. No part of this publication may be reproduced in any form or by any means (including photocopying or storing it in any medium by electronic means and whether or not transiently or incidentally to some other use of this publication) without the written permission of the copyright owner, except in accordance with the provisions of the Copyright, Designs and Patents Act 1988 or under the terms of a licence issued by the Copyright Licensing Agency, Saffron House, 6–10 Kirby Street, London EC1N 8TS (www.cla.co.uk). Applications for the copyright owner's written permission should be addressed to the publisher.

Edited by Rebecca Rissman, Daniel Nunn, and Catherine Veitch
Designed by Philippa Jenkins
Picture research by Elizabeth Alexander
Production by Helen McCreath
Originated by Capstone Global Library Ltd
Printed and bound in China

ISBN 978 1 4062 7149 2
17 16 15 14 13
10 9 8 7 6 5 4 3 2 1

British Library Cataloguing in Publication Data
A full catalogue record for this book is available from the British Library.

Acknowledgements
We would like to thank the following for permission to reproduce photographs: Alamy pp. 9 (© Kuttig – People), 23 (© Kuttig – People); Corbis pp. 6 (© Hulton-Deutsch Collection), 11 (© Auslöser), 12 (© E.O. Hoppe), 18 (© Hulton-Deutsch Collection), 21 (© Ariel Skelley/Blend Images), 23 (© Hulton-Deutsch Collection); Getty Images pp. 4 (Fox Photos), 8 (Harold M. Lambert), 10 (Richards/Fox Photos), 14 (Fox Photos), 15 (Jade Lee/Asia Images), 19 (OJO Images RF), 20 (FPG/Hulton Archive), 22 (Lambert), 23 (Harold M. Lambert), 23 (Richards/Fox Photos); Shutterstock pp. 7 (© Blend Images), 13 (© Golden Pixels LLC); Superstock pp. 5 (Marka), 16, 17 (Cultura Limited).

Front cover photographs of boys playing marbles, 1920s, reproduced with permission of Getty Images (H. Armstrong Roberts/Retrofile), and boys playing handheld video games reproduced with permission of Getty Images (Tanya Constantine/Blend Images). Back cover photograph of a boy on a rocking horse, with his mother and sister beside him reproduced with permission of Superstock.

We would like to thank Nancy Harris and Diana Bentley for their invaluable help in the preparation of this book.

Every effort has been made to contact copyright holders of material reproduced in this book. Any omissions will be rectified in subsequent printings if notice is given to the publisher.

Contents

Comparing the past and present

Things in the past have already happened.

Things in the present are happening now.

Playing with friends has changed over time.

The way children play with friends today is very different to the past.

Games

In the past children played simple games. Some children played marbles.

Today, some children play
computer games.

Entertainment

In the past children listened to stories on the radio.

Today, many children watch television.

Playing outdoors

In the past children swam in rivers or lakes.

Always swim with an adult.

Today, most children swim in swimming pools.

In the past some children wore roller skates.

Today, many children wear
roller blades.

Toys

metal

In the past most children's toys were made of metal or wood.

plastic

Today, most children's toys are made of plastic.

In the past many toys were handmade.

Today, most toys are made by machines in factories.

Friends far away

In the past some children wrote letters to friends who lived far away.

Today, some children use a
computer to talk to friends
and family who live far away.

Then and now

In the past children played skipping games with their friends. Today, children still play skipping games!

Picture glossary

computer games electronic games played on a computer or TV

handmade something that is made by a person and not by a machine

marbles small glass toys that are rolled in a simple game

radio machine that plays music, news and stories

Index

Notes for parents and teachers

Before reading

Talk to children about the difference between the past and present. Explain that the word *past* refers to things that have already happened. The word *present* refers to things that are happening now. Ask children to describe what they did yesterday or earlier in the day, and then explain that those activities took place in the past.

After reading

- Explain that the way children played with their friends has changed over time. Ask children to name their favourite things to do with their friends. Make a list of the activities on the board. Then, go down the list and tell children which activities would not have been possible in the past.

- Turn to pages 8–9 and explain that technology has changed the way children play over time.

- Encourage children to think of activities they enjoy doing with their friends today that would have been similar in the past. For example, skipping and playing hide-and-seek are activities that have changed very little over time.